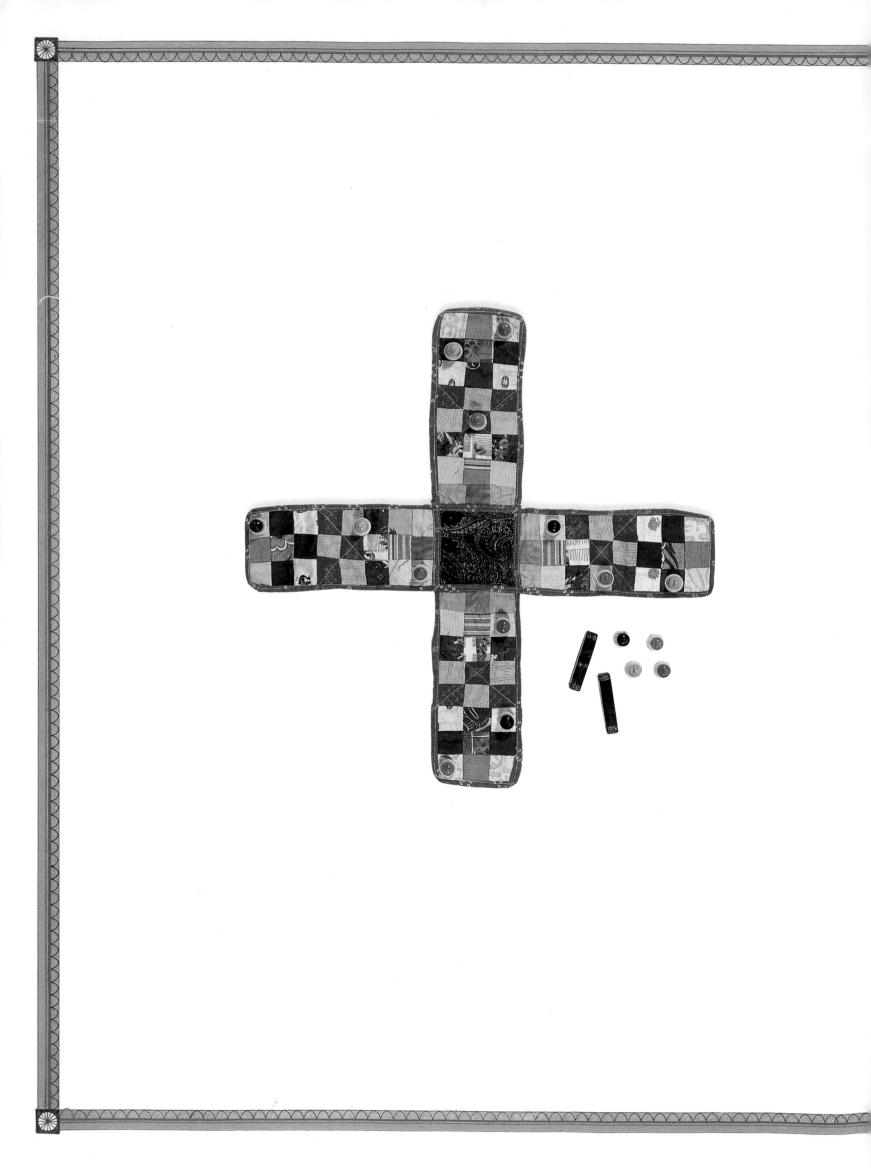

H·O·W
CHILDREN
L·I·V·E·D

Written by Chris and Melanie Rice

Illustrated by Sergio

DK

LONDON, NEW YORK, MUNICH,
MELBOURNE, and DELHI

Project Editor Dawn Sirett
Art Editor Jane Horne
Production Marguerite Fenn
Picture Research Lorna Ainger
U.S. Editor Camela Decaire

Managing Editor Jane Yorke
Managing Art Editors Gillian Allan and Chris Scollen

Consultants Dr. David Allan, Dr. Barbara Brend,
Clara Chastan, Christopher Gravett, Gordon C. Hamilton,
Dr. Nicholas James, Dr. Simon James, Jonathan King,
Professor Robert Layton, Shelby Mamdani,
Carol Michaelson, and Anne Pearson

First American edition, 1995
Paperback edition, 2005
05 06 07 08 09 10 9 8 7 6 5 4 3 2 1

Published in the United States by
DK Publishing, Inc., 375 Hudson Street
New York, New York 10014

A catalog record for this book is available from the Library of Congress.

ISBN 0-7566-1806-1

Printed and bound in Slovakia, TBB

Discover more at
www.dk.com

Contents

Children Around the World

This book tells you what life was like for 16 children living at different times in history. You can see where each child lived on this world map. It shows modern continent names because many of the place names the children knew have changed.

As you read about the children, compare the foods that they ate, what they wore, and the games that they played. How different are their lives from yours today?

Pierrette was living in France about 200 years ago. *"My brother and I live on the streets and beg for food."*

Anne was living in Britain about 160 years ago. *"I help my father who is a station master. I show train passengers to their cars."*

NORTH AMERICA

EUROPE

AFRICA

SOUTH AMERICA

Sancho was living in Spain about 550 years ago. *"My home is a castle and when I grow up, I want to be a knight."*

Ohe-tika-wi was living on the Great Plains of North America about 150 years ago. *"I help my mother in the camp and am learning to decorate buffalo skins."*

Jack was living in the United States of America about 70 years ago. *"I am a class monitor at school and help out in my family drugstore."*

Xochitl was living in Mexico about 500 years ago. *"I help my mother at home. We make delicious tortillas."*

Bilal was living in West Africa about 600 years ago. *"I was sold as a servant to some traveling merchants."*

Asa was living in Norway about 1,050 years ago. "Every day I get up at sunrise to milk the cows and goats on our family farm."

Vitalinus was living in Germany about 1,900 years ago. "I help my father who works as a scribe near a Roman fort."

Giovanna was living in Italy some 500 years ago. "I live in a large palace and am learning to read Latin, play music, and write poetry."

Lysander was living in Greece about 2,500 years ago. "I go to school and am learning the potter's craft from my father."

ASIA

Ichiro was living in Japan about 350 years ago. "I'm learning how to fight and follow the samurai code of honor."

Miao was living in China about 2,100 years ago. "I am a servant in the emperor's palace."

Wiliyati was living in Australia about 300 years ago. "I live in the desert and can find water in hidden pools."

AUSTRALASIA

Hori was living in Egypt about 3,200 years ago. "I am learning to be a scribe and will train for many years."

Kumar was living in India about 400 years ago. "I live near the emperor's palace and help look after the royal elephants."

Find out about history
Turn the page to learn more about history and each of these children. On page 42, you can discover how we find out about the past and see the children on a timeline. On page 44, a glossary explains history words, and on page 45, there is a pronunciation guide for the unusual words and names in the book.

Sleeping on the roof
On hot summer nights, I keep cool by going up to the roof to sleep.

Shaving hair
My sister, Merit, has her hair shaved by a servant so that she can keep cool.

Growing Up in Ancient Egypt

Hori was born in Egypt in 1200 BC and is now nine years old. Hori is the son of a skilled tomb artist. He is learning to be a scribe. As most people cannot read or write, they have to pay scribes to write official letters for them.

Sunshade on roof

Walled garden

Hori's home
Hori lives in a large house with two floors. Like most Egyptian houses, it is made of mud bricks.

Hori
Hori doesn't wear many clothes because it's very hot for much of the year. Like other Egyptian boys, his hair is shaved except for a single lock.

Whitewashed walls

Granaries for storing grain

Front rooms used for entertaining and conducting business

Raised floors to keep snakes from getting in

Entrance

Kitchen

Clay balls

Windows

Clay spinning tops

Hori's toys
Hori likes to play ball games. His sister often plays with her doll or spinning tops.

Servants' quarters

Playing
After lessons, we have time to play. This game is one of my favorites. We throw and catch balls while riding piggyback! My friends are playing tug-of-war.

Tug-of-war

Playing senet
Up on the roof, my grandparents are playing a board game called "senet."

Servants bring fish and beer for lunch.

Hori's training
Hori is learning Egyptian picture writing, which is called "hieroglyphics." He will train for many years. Royal tomb artists, like Hori's father, paint hieroglyphs (individual pictures) on monuments, temples, tombs, and religious papers. For things such as letters and stories, scribes use a quickly written form of hieroglyphics called "hieratic" script.

Hieratic script

Hieroglyphs

Egyptian writing on papyrus (paper made from reeds)

Painted scenes

Hori's village
Hori lives near the Nile River, the longest river in the world. Skilled craftspeople, like Hori's father, live here, and farmers grow crops in the fertile land next to the river.

Clay beads for hair

Wooden doll

Reed brushes for writing

Wooden paint palette

Paint pigments

Paint pigments
Hori's father uses paints made from ground-up pigments. Charcoal makes black. Minerals, like cobalt, make blue and other colors.

Hori's lessons
Hori practices his writing with his cousin. They use wooden paint palettes and reed brushes.

Brush for painting large hieroglyphs

Picture writing
Each hieroglyph stands for a sound. We spell words by putting several pictures together. These hieroglyphs stand for these letter sounds:

M   J   D   P

Dressing
Our slave helps me dress in the morning. My tunic is fastened with a belt and a brooch at both shoulders.

Praying
There is an altar to the goddess Athena in our courtyard. We say prayers to her every day.

Shopping
After school, I walk through the market. Merchants come from the port of Piraeus and farmers from nearby villages.

Growing Up in Ancient Greece

It is 500 BC in the city of Athens. Lysander works here as an apprentice potter to his father, Demetrius. He is nine years old and has been going to school for two years.

Lyre

Lysander
Lysander wears a short tunic called a "chiton." His mother makes clothes for everyone in the family.

Empty tortoiseshell sound box

One of a pair of double pipes

A slave takes Lysander to school and waits to take him home.

Teacher

Lysander practices his writing.

Learning
Lysander has learned to read and write at school. He can recite the poetry of Homer and count on an abacus. He has also learned to play the lyre and double pipes (two pipes that are blown at the same time).

Lysander's house
In the center of Athens, close to the "agora," or marketplace, is the busy potter's quarter. Lysander and his family live here above a pottery. At the front of the house is the pottery shop.

All kinds of customers come to the shop. Some are merchants who will sell Demetrius's pots in far-off lands.

Market stalls

Pottery shop

Cerberus
I keep an eye on my dog, Cerberus, in the pottery workshop. He might knock over the pots!

Dinner
Our slave cooks dinner. Usually there is barley porridge with olives and salad.

Lysander's work

Lysander learns the potter's craft by watching his father. Sometimes he is allowed to turn the wheel, but he must be careful to keep it steady or the pot will lose its shape.

The pots are fired (baked) in a large oven called a "kiln."

Painted dish for food

Lysander's father turns the potter's wheel.

Lysander helps mix a black clay solution. This will be used for paint.

Pots, jugs, and vases

All sorts of things are made in the pottery workshop: jugs, vases, pots, lamps, cups – even babies' bottles and toys.

Toy horses and riders made with leftover clay

Painted vase showing people gathering olives

Playing
After dinner, I like to play outside with my friends. Sometimes we roll hoops.

Washing
I wash by pouring oil over my body and scraping off dirt with a scraper. Then I rinse with cold water.

Palace walls

Emperor's palace

Growing Up in Ancient China

It is 130 BC in the empire of "All Under Heaven." Miao is a maid to Lady Wang. Lady Wang is the mother of the emperor, Wu, who is in the eleventh year of his reign. Miao and Lady Wang live in the palace with the emperor and his nobles.

The palace
The people of the city are not allowed to set eyes on Emperor Wu, so the palace is surrounded by high walls. Miao never leaves the palace grounds.

Miao
Miao wears a long, loose robe with wide sleeves. She combs her hair with a small wooden comb and ties it back to keep it tidy.

Small wooden comb

Bronze mirror decorated with patterns (back of mirror shown)

Toiletry box
Miao keeps Lady Wang's combs, makeup, and hair ornaments in a round toiletry box.

Dressing Lady Wang
Miao looks after Lady Wang's clothes and helps her dress. Lady Wang puts on one of her many silk gowns. Miao spends a long time arranging Lady Wang's hair in front of a bronze mirror until both of them are happy. Finally, she powders and rouges Lady Wang's cheeks.

Embroidery
I embroider beautiful designs on silk gowns for Lady Wang. If I make a mistake, I pick out the thread and start again.

Dancing
After dinner, I dance to entertain Lady Wang. Musicians accompany me on the pipes and zither.

Serving Lady Wang

Miao brings Lady Wang dinner on a tray. Lady Wang eats from lacquered tableware using chopsticks. Miao serves her stewed meats with vegetables, taro, water chestnuts, sticky rice cakes, and winter melon.

Chopsticks

Lacquered wooden tableware

Small bowls

Water chestnuts

Lacquered wooden cup

Winter melon

Taro root

Lacquered toiletry box

Eating dinner

Lady Wang sits on a bamboo mat on the floor and eats from a low table.

A gift for the emperor

When Lady Wang goes to see Emperor Wu, Miao accompanies her. Lady Wang has a gift for the emperor – a belt hook in the shape of a tiger for fastening his silk robes.

Bronze belt hook

The emperor
When Lady Wang asks to see the emperor, I go with her. We must bow low in the presence of Emperor Wu.

I like to look at the emperor's clothes. They are made of the very finest silk.

Growing Up in the Roman Empire

In AD 120 the Roman army is busy strengthening its defenses along the Rhine River in what is now called Germany. Vitalinus and his family live outside a fort. Vitalinus helps his father, Genialis, who is a retired soldier. Genialis now works as a scribe for people who cannot read or write.

Roman coins

The fort

Hundreds of Roman soldiers live inside the strong stone fort. Genialis's shop is one of the many shops and houses built outside the fort walls.

Genialis writes on vellum (prepared animal skin) with a pen and ink.

Vitalinus

Vitalinus plays soldiers with his wooden sword. When it is cold, he wears a hooded cape and leather boots.

The soldiers bring their letters and documents.

Sliding bolts in the lid (shown turned over)

A strongbox

Genialis keeps the money he earns as a scribe under lock and key in a strongbox.

Strongbox

The scribe's shop

The soldiers of the twenty-second legion come to Genialis's shop and pay him to help them with reading or writing. Vitalinus gives his father some vellum and a pen.

Prayers
Every evening, my father offers prayers to the "lares," or spirits, who protect our house.

Supper
After prayers, my family has supper together. Tonight there are meatballs made from sheep's brains, eggs, and herbs.

16

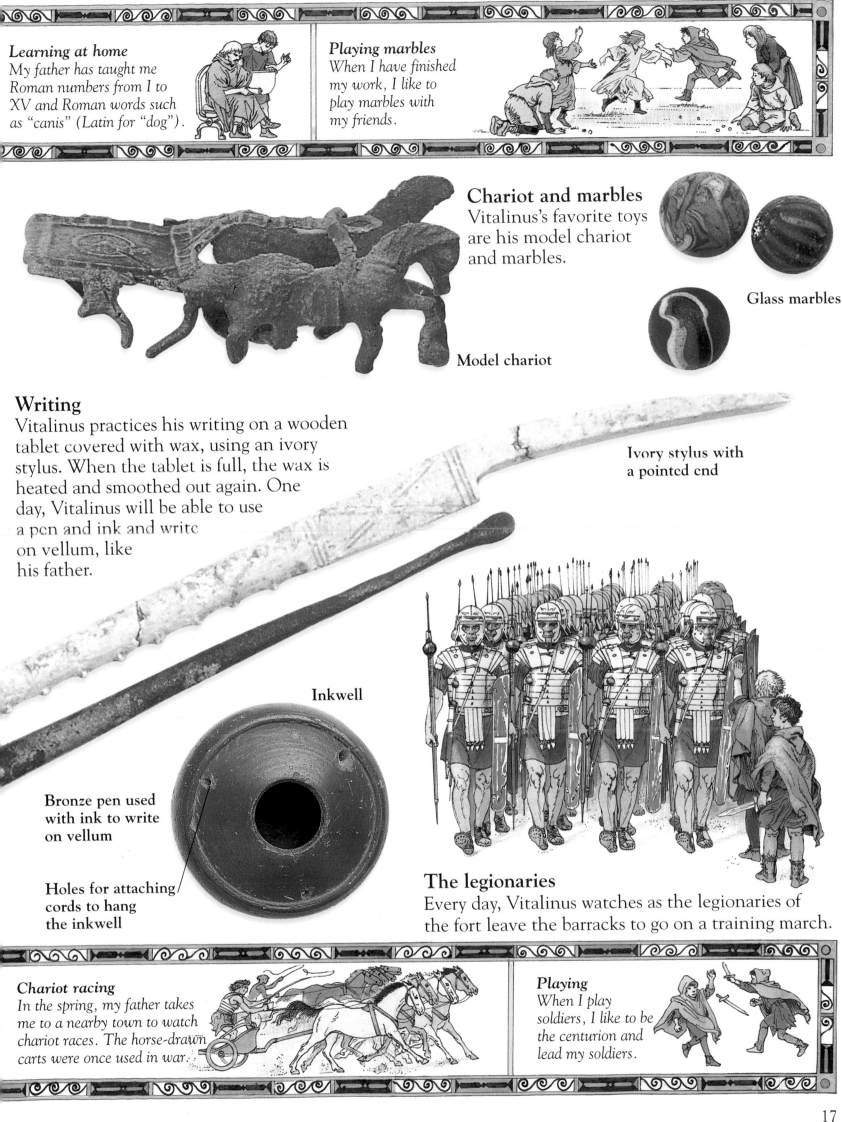

Learning at home
My father has taught me Roman numbers from I to XV and Roman words such as "canis" (Latin for "dog").

Playing marbles
When I have finished my work, I like to play marbles with my friends.

Chariot and marbles
Vitalinus's favorite toys are his model chariot and marbles.

Glass marbles

Model chariot

Writing
Vitalinus practices his writing on a wooden tablet covered with wax, using an ivory stylus. When the tablet is full, the wax is heated and smoothed out again. One day, Vitalinus will be able to use a pen and ink and write on vellum, like his father.

Ivory stylus with a pointed end

Inkwell

Bronze pen used with ink to write on vellum

Holes for attaching cords to hang the inkwell

The legionaries
Every day, Vitalinus watches as the legionaries of the fort leave the barracks to go on a training march.

Chariot racing
In the spring, my father takes me to a nearby town to watch chariot races. The horse-drawn carts were once used in war.

Playing
When I play soldiers, I like to be the centurion and lead my soldiers.

17

Longboat   Fjord

Forge

Asa's farm

Growing Up in Viking Norway

It is AD 950 in Norway. Asa lives with her family on a farm near the shores of Hardanger Fjord. Depending on the time of year, she sows seeds, gathers vegetables, or grinds corn to make flour.

The farmhouse
The long farmhouse has one main room for cooking, eating, and sleeping. There is also a food storage room and a dayroom for sewing and weaving. The main living area has room for grandparents, aunts, and uncles. Asa helps her mother with the cooking.

When no one is looking, Asa takes a sip from the stew.

Asa
In Norway the winters are long and cold. Asa wears a woolen skirt and fur vest to keep warm, and leather boots tied with straps.

Cooking pots

Thralls
Asa's family owns two thralls (slaves) who help with the household chores.

Boat brooch

Silver locket

Amulet and brooch
Asa wears a locket around her neck. It is her amulet (lucky charm). She also has a brooch shaped like her father's longboat, which she uses to fasten her cloak in snowy weather.

Cooking cauldron
Asa's favorite meal is meat stew. It is cooked over the fire in a huge iron cauldron, supported by a tripod. There's enough to feed the whole family.

Milking
I work hard on the farm. At sunrise, I milk the cows. The milk is made into butter and cheese at the dairy.

The longboat
Every spring my father and the other men sail east in their longboat.

Tongs for holding
hot iron on
an anvil

Wooden handle

Saw made in a
Viking forge

Iron blade

Leather shoe

Ice-skating
Asa and her friends
go ice-skating in the
winter. Asa's skates
are like this one.
They use bones
for blades.

Bone blade

Making tools
Asa often visits her uncle, Bjorn,
who makes tools, weapons, and
jewelry in his forge. He
hammers the metal into
shape on an iron
block called
an anvil.

Iron
handle

Tongs

Anvil

Wooden board
that may have
been used for
hneftafl

One of the
tripod's
three legs

Game pieces fit
into 49 holes
in the board.

Iron cauldron

Pronged feet were stuck
in the floor to keep the
cauldron stable.

Games
Asa likes to play "hneftafl," a
game a lot like chess. She must
use her pieces to protect the king.

Skating
In winter, when
the rivers freeze
over, I like to
go ice-skating.

Snowball
fights
When it snows,
my friends and
I can have
snowball fights.

Hneftafl
During the long
winter evenings,
I play hneftafl
with my brother.

*The men load the boat
with furs, jewelry,
and salted fish.*

*In the East
they will trade
their goods for
silks, spices, and
embroidered cloth.*

Telling stories
*At night we sit around
the fire and listen to
sagas (stories) of
brave heroes.*

Sold as a servant
I lived in Taghaza until my parents died. Then I was sold to traveling merchants from Morocco.

Setting up camp
At the end of a hot day's traveling through the desert, we set up camp. I serve the merchants a drink of water mixed with millet and a little honey.

Growing Up in the Mali Empire

It is 1400 in the West African Empire of Mali. Bilal was born in Taghaza, a major salt-mining center of the Sahara Desert. He is nine years old and has been sold as a servant to Arab merchants from North Africa. The merchants are traveling south to Timbuktu to trade their goods in the busy market.

Bilal
Bilal wears a loose cotton robe that helps keep him cool in the heat of the desert.

Cotton robe

Timbuktu

Crossing the desert
Bilal and the Arab merchants have spent many days crossing the Sahara Desert. The merchants use an astrolabe to navigate their way. They are now nearing the city of Timbuktu and can see it in the distance.

Astrolabes like this were used to mark the position of the stars.

Traveling by camel
The merchants are traveling to Timbuktu by camel. The camels carry the merchants' goods: salt from the desert mines at Taghaza, perfumes, cloth, and fine books for the famous library at Timbuktu. Bilal helps lead the camels.

Feeding the camels
I help the other servants feed the camels. I give them a block of salt to lick – a real treat!

A fever
Today one of the camels is sick. The merchants think it might be a fever spread by blood-sucking flies.

20

A waterhole
We stop to collect more water at a waterhole, where rainwater rises near the surface of the land. The merchants order me to fetch them a drink.

Clay pot for carrying drinking water

At Timbuktu market

Bilal works hard, fetching and carrying for his masters. On arriving in Timbuktu, he helps take their goods to the market. The merchants trade their wares for gold, kola nuts, ostrich feathers, and cowrie shells, which the West Africans bring in from areas south of Timbuktu. This trade has made the West Africans very rich.

Timbuktu market

The merchants' goods are strapped to the camels.

Cowrie shells

Cowrie shells are used as money by the traders.

Bilal walks on foot, leading his master's camel.

Cowrie shells

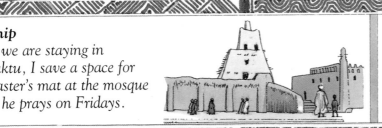

Worship
While we are staying in Timbuktu, I save a space for my master's mat at the mosque where he prays on Fridays.

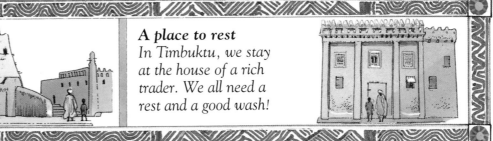

A place to rest
In Timbuktu, we stay at the house of a rich trader. We all need a rest and a good wash!

21

Charging with a lance
In jousts, knights fight one-on-one on horseback, knocking each other to the ground with lances. To practice, I aim my lance at a tilting post.

If I don't ride by quickly enough, the swinging weight will knock me off my horse.

Growing Up in a Spanish Castle

It is 1450 and Sancho is learning the skills of war. Already he can saddle a horse, wield a sword, and throw a javelin. He lives with his uncle, Don Pedro, who is a fierce warrior. Sancho hopes that one day he, too, will become a "caballero," or knight, and ride into battle.

The castle
Sancho lives in a castle high on a hill. The castle is surrounded by thick stone walls.

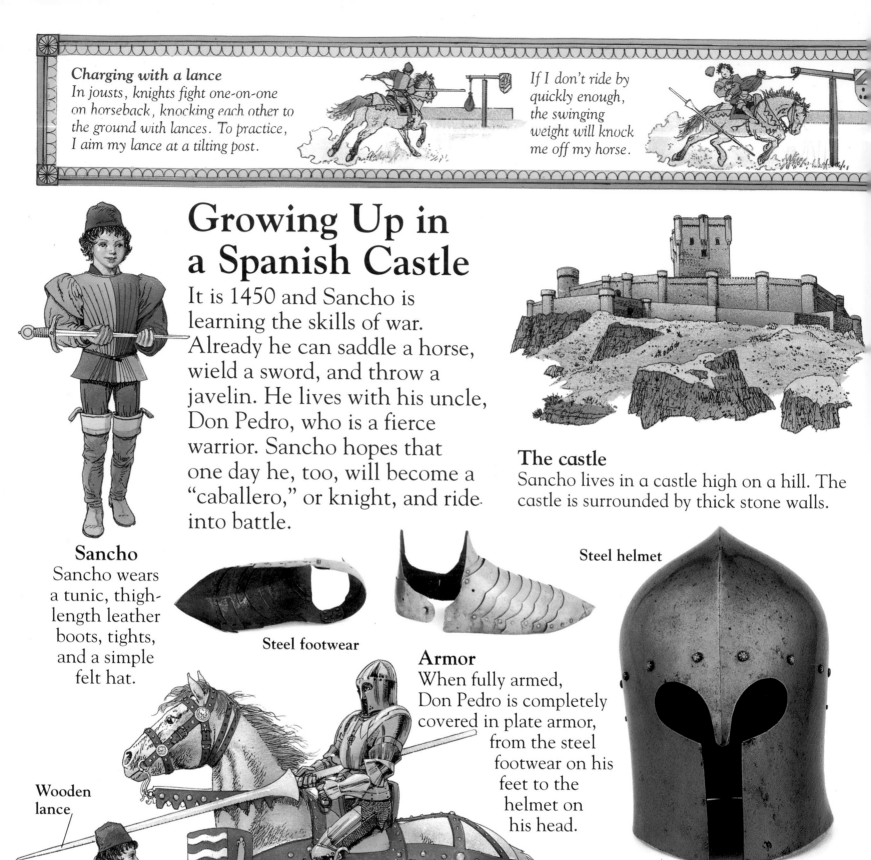

Sancho
Sancho wears a tunic, thigh-length leather boots, tights, and a simple felt hat.

Steel footwear

Steel helmet

Armor
When fully armed, Don Pedro is completely covered in plate armor, from the steel footwear on his feet to the helmet on his head.

Wooden lance

Shield

Helping Don Pedro
Sancho chooses the right saddle and bridle for Don Pedro's horse and then helps Don Pedro put on his armor. He knows how all the parts of a suit of armor fit together.

Sports
I like wrestling, stone putting, and acrobatics, but my favorite sport is archery.

Mealtimes
At mealtimes, Sancho is expected to carve the meat at the table, serve Don Pedro with his wine cup and dinner plate, and watch his manners!

Dinner plate

Serving food
Sancho serves the food with broad-bladed knives like these.

Broad blades

Central design based on a coat of arms, or family symbol

Learning
Fighting is only one part of a knight's training. I am also taught to read, write, and count by the castle priest.

Entertainment
While the knights eat, visiting entertainers called "minstrels" sing, play music, and tell stories.

Minstrels

Bedtime
I sleep on a bed of straw in the Great Hall with the other boys. At dawn, we get up for mass.

Carved figure

Wooden saddle, decorated with carvings, used for special occasions, such as parades

Music
Music forms an important part of castle entertainment. Sancho is learning to play the lute. This modern lute is similar to the one he would have played.

Lute

Getting up
In the morning, a servant wakes me up and helps me dress.

Mass
From my bedroom, I can hear the church bells of Santa Maria Novella. We go to mass there on Sundays and saints' days.

Growing Up in Renaissance Italy

It is 1490 in the city of Florence. Giovanna lives with her family in a large palace with many servants. She is learning all the accomplishments of a lady. Her father, Francesco, has paid an artist to paint portraits of his wife and three children.

Giovanna
Giovanna wears a long velvet dress with wide sleeves, a simple headdress, and a pendant around her neck.

Printed book

Enameled gold and pearl pendant

Giovanna's possessions
Giovanna's favorite possessions are her pendant, jewelry box, and printed storybook. Until recently, all books were handwritten.

Jewelry box

Giovanna's home
Florence
Giovanna's father is a wealthy banker and runs his business from the palace, which is in the center of Florence.

Flute

Lute

Giovanna's education
Giovanna and her sister are taught at home by a tutor. They have learned to sing, play musical instruments, write poetry, and read Latin. They are also being taught how to run a household.

Table manners
In addition to knives, we now have forks to eat with. Sometimes I still use my fingers by mistake.

Walking in the gardens
I like to walk in our gardens with my mother and look at the statues along the paths.

24

Fine clothes

Mother shows me the new dress that I am to wear when I have my portrait painted. It is made of embroidered cloth.

Singing madrigals

Sometimes, after dinner, my sister and I sing a song called a "madrigal" for my father's friends.

Easel

Sketch

The portrait

Giovanna sits for her portrait with her sister and her baby brother. She wears her new dress.

Giovanna's mother

The artist has already finished the portrait of Giovanna's mother. She is a fine singer and is shown holding a music book. Francesco is proud to show the picture to all his friends.

Giovanna's footwear

Giovanna wears a pair of pattens over her shoes. The pattens raise her feet off the ground and protect her shoes from the dirt.

Pattens

Furniture

Giovanna's baby brother has the same cradle that she slept in as a baby. Like other furniture in the palace, it is decorated with beautiful carvings.

Carved wooden cradle

Rocking the baby

If I'm very quiet, our nurse lets me rock my younger brother to sleep in his cradle.

Farm on an artificial island

Growing Up in Aztec Mexico

It is 1500 in North America, but in the calendar Xochitl uses, the year is 8 Flint. Xochitl helps with the work around her family home. Her people believe that one day the sun will die and crops will not grow, but today the sun is in the sky. Xochitl gives thanks.

Xochitl
Xochitl makes her clothes with her mother. She wears a long blouse, a skirt made of cactus fiber, and cactus fiber shoes.

The farm
Xochitl lives in a village on the shore of a lake. Her family farm stands across the water on an artificial island built with fertile mud from the lake.

Avocado

Tomato

Red and green chili peppers

Xochitl pats the dough into tortillas.

Heavy stone roller to grind corn

Dried corn kernels

Grinding stone

Preparing food
Xochitl's mother grinds corn into flour on a grinding stone, while Xochitl makes tortillas (pancakes) for the family dinner. She fills them with beans, peppers, tomatoes, and avocados.

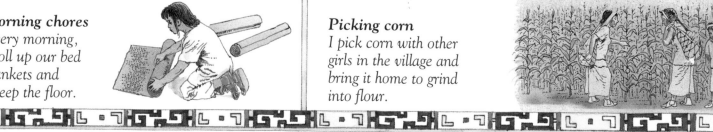

Morning chores
Every morning, I roll up our bed blankets and sweep the floor.

Picking corn
I pick corn with other girls in the village and bring it home to grind into flour.

Making clothes
Xochitl and her mother weave thread into cloth using a wooden back-strap loom. The thread they use is made from cactus fiber, spun on a spindle.

Needle case

Spindle with spun thread wound around it

Pins and needles
Thorns from the maguey make perfect pins and needles for weaving and sewing. Xochitl is careful not to stab her fingers on the sharp thorns.

Cactus needles

Loom bar is attached to a tree or post.

Back-strap loom

Long threads are called the warp.

Weaving sword used to smooth down weft threads

Weft threads run under and over warp threads.

Corn

Strap fits around weaver's waist.

Crops
Corn, tomatoes, chili peppers, and avocados are grown on Xochitl's family farm.

Traveling by canoe
Every day, my father and brothers travel across the lake by canoe to reach our farm on the artificial island.

Spinning thread
My sister and I spin cactus fiber on a spindle to make thread.

Cactus leaves
My father collects maguey leaves, which we use to make thread and paper. We use the cactus thorns for pins and needles.

Music
My brother plays his flute for the corn goddess, so that she will help the crops grow.

Washing the elephants
Every day, I help the elephant keepers lead the elephants to the Jumna River. We wash the elephants in the river.

Feeding the elephants
We feed the elephants leafy branches. As a special treat, I give my favorite elephant, Gajpati, some cooked rice.

Growing Up in Moghul India

City of Agra — Emperor's palace — Stables — Houses

It is 1600 in India, during the reign of the emperor Akbar. Kumar lives in the city of Agra. He works as an assistant to his father, who is one of the royal elephant keepers.

Kumar
Kumar wears a simple tunic over a pair of pants and a turban on his head.

Elephant bonnet

This is the type of cloth that the elephants would have worn on their backs.

Kumar's home
Kumar lives in a small house in the city, close to the palace of the emperor. Near the house are the stables where the royal elephants are kept.

Royal musicians

The bonnet is decorated with stars and a crescent.

Brightly colored fringe

Patterned border

Elephant trappings
When the elephants are to appear in a royal procession, the elephant keepers dress them in special trappings. Kumar helps put colorful bonnets on their heads and richly woven cloths on their backs.

The musicians
Kumar cheers as Emperor Akbar's musicians pass by in the procession. They are famous throughout India.

Shopping
My mother goes to the market to buy food. The shopkeepers also sell pots, knives, and other goods.

Cooking
My sister makes chapati (bread), which we eat with hot, spicy dishes.

Games

At home, Kumar likes to play pachisi with his sister. Pachisi is a board game like Parcheesi. It is still played in India today.

Modern pachisi cloth board

Glass counters

Patchwork cloth of different colors

Food

Kumar follows the principles of Hinduism and chooses to be a vegetarian. He likes rice, peas, limes, lentils, and spices.

Lentils

Coriander

Peas

Limes

Ginger

Emperor Akbar

A royal procession

When Emperor Akbar returns home to the city, there is a spectacular procession. The emperor rides his favorite horse. Kumar proudly watches Gajpati and the other elephants as they pass by.

Elephants dressed in special trappings

Wrestling
I like to wrestle with my friends. I pretend to be the famous wrestler Jag Sobha.

Watching polo
After dinner, I watch a polo match over the palace wall. The ball is made of smoldering wood so the players can see it in the dark.

Playing
My friends and I are learning to play a board game called "go." You have to capture and surround your opponent's pieces.

Archery
Archery is my favorite sport. Our tutor says that I am the best in my class at hitting the target.

Growing Up in Tokugawa Japan

It is 1650 in Japan. Ichiro is training to be a samurai warrior like his father. One day he will fight for his overlord, the Tokugawa shogun. He must also learn to write, dance, and play music, and to be polite and honorable. Above all, he must be loyal and obedient to the shogun.

Shogun's castle

Moat

Life in Edo
Ichiro lives near the shogun's castle in Edo (now called Tokyo), the capital city of Japan. The castle is surrounded by a moat. Most of the houses in Edo have walls made of paper and wood.

Ichiro
Ichiro wears a kimono. He has a pair of samurai pants called "hakama," which he wears over his kimono.

Japanese calligraphy

Ichiro and his sisters sit on straw mats called "tatami."

Japanese calligraphy
Ichiro is learning the art of Japanese calligraphy – a style of writing that is painted with a brush and ink.

Poetry
Poetry is also part of a samurai's training. Ichiro and his sisters like to read and write poetry in the rock garden at the side of their house.

Ties wrap around the waist to fasten the pants.

Hakama

Hakama
When I was seven years old, I was given my first pair of hakama. I wear these pants on special occasions.

Learning calligraphy
My tutor is teaching me Japanese calligraphy. I'm learning many new characters. I try to paint each one quickly and accurately.

30

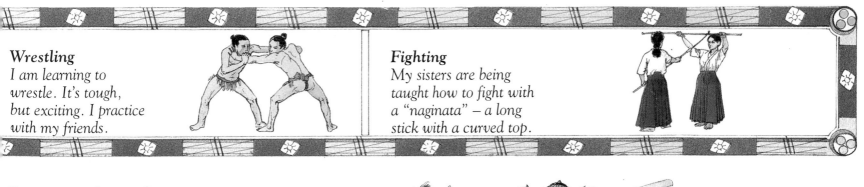

Wrestling
*I am learning to
wrestle. It's tough,
but exciting. I practice
with my friends.*

Fighting
*My sisters are being
taught how to fight with
a "naginata" – a long
stick with a curved top.*

Learning from the masters

Ichiro and his friends often go to watch
some of the master samurai practicing
their skills at fighting. The samurai use
both hands to wield their long, heavy
swords, or "katana." They also carry
a short sword called a "wakizashi."

Samurai armor

Ichiro admires the fine armor
of the samurai. It is made of
tough strips of leather or
iron, which hang from the
body on strings. A "kabuto,"
or helmet, protects
the head
and face.

Samurai swords

Ichiro will be given a
wakizashi like this one
when he is fifteen. He
will also receive a katana.

Wakizashi
sword

Lacquered
iron kabuto
(samurai
helmet)

Neck guard made
of iron plates
laced together
with silk

Pottery bowls
for serving tea

Serving tea

Tea ceremonies are an important
part of samurai social life. Ichiro's father
serves green tea to his guests in small bowls.

Tea ceremony
*My father sometimes holds a ceremony in the tea
house in the garden. Afterward, the guests rise,
bow, and tuck any leftover sweetmeats into their
wide sleeves. It is rude to leave any food behind.*

31

Spear throwing
I like to practice spear throwing.
If one of my brothers throws
a piece of bark in the air, I
can hit it right in the middle.

Making fire
To start a fire, I rub a
stick against some soft
wood, causing sparks
that set dry grass on fire.

Growing Up in an Australian Desert

In 1700 Wiliyati's people, the Pitjantjatjara, are living near Uluru, a great rock that seems to change color magically as the sun moves across the sky. Uluru is at the center of a country that will one day be called Australia.

Uluru

Wiliyati

Wiliyati wears very little because it is so hot in the desert. When he is older, he hopes to wear a necklace and fur tassels like his father.

Hair strings with fur tassels, worn as an ornament

Kangaroo tooth necklace

On the move

Wiliyati's people travel the desert, following in the footsteps of their ancestors. When they set up camp, they build a windbreak and make a fire.

Wiliyati and his friends try to catch a lizard. Wiliyati aims his spear at it.

Living in the desert

Wiliyati can live quite happily in the desert. He finds his way using emu tracks, trees, and hills, and can catch lizards as they dart between rocks.

Making flour
My sister helps my mother make flour
by grinding grass seeds between two
stones. They mix the flour with water
and bake it in a fire to make bread.

Finding water
I find water in hidden
pools and quench my
thirst with sweet-tasting
roots called "ungka."

32

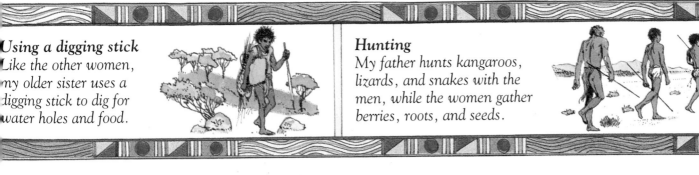

Using a digging stick
Like the other women, my older sister uses a digging stick to dig for water holes and food.

Hunting
My father hunts kangaroos, lizards, and snakes with the men, while the women gather berries, roots, and seeds.

Paintings
Wiliyati's people paint pictures about the Dreamtime, when their ancestors roamed the earth, on rocks and caves at Uluru. The patterns on this modern Aboriginal painting are similar to the ones that Wiliyati's people painted.

Dreamtime
The men and women tell Wiliyati and the other children some of the stories about the Dreamtime. They draw patterns in the sand to mark their ancestors' tracks. When the children are older, they will be told more about the Dreamtime.

Windbreak

Patterns in sand

Wooden boomerang

Tools
Wiliyati carries a small spear. When he is older, he will use a boomerang and spear thrower and go hunting with the men.

Curved sides enable the thrower to be used as a bowl as well.

Wooden spear thrower – used as a lever to throw a spear and give it more speed

Using a boomerang
My father uses his boomerang for many different jobs. He hunts animals with it.

Digging
He digs pits for earth ovens with his boomerang.

Scraping
He can also use it to scrape hot ashes over meat when he cooks meat in an earth oven.

Sleeping on the streets
Each night, we have to look for somewhere new to sleep. I tell Joseph bedtime stories to comfort him.

Breakfast
I share some bread with Joseph for breakfast. Some people say the bakers make the poor people's bread with chalk instead of flour.

Growing Up in France Before the Revolution

It is 1789 in Paris, the capital city of France. Many poor people are starving and talk of revolution. Pierrette and her brother Joseph are homeless orphans. Their mother and father both died of a fever. The children have to beg for food.

Life in Paris
Pierrette and Joseph live on the streets of Paris. Many other people who can't afford to rent rooms also have to sleep out in the open.

Pierrette
Pierrette has no shoes and her only dress is very ragged. She doesn't know what she will do when it wears out.

Pierrette and Joseph beg for bread.

Embroidered purse

Painted buttons

Sou coin

A lost purse
Once the children were very lucky. They found a purse with 15 sous inside – the price of a loaf of bread.

Buttons
When the children's mother died, they kept two buttons from her best dress to remember her by.

Begging
Pierrette and Joseph beg for food at the market. Pierrette has noticed that very few carts now bring food from the countryside and some days the baker's shop stays shut and there is no bread at all.

Lemonade stall

34

Revolutionary talk
People complain that we do not get enough food. They say things might get better if there is a revolution.

The market
I often take Joseph to the market. Sometimes we find some old fruit or scraps to eat.

The Palais Royal

To cheer themselves up, Pierrette and Joseph go to their favorite place – the Palais Royal. Here there are magic lantern shows, puppet shows, musicians, acrobats, lemonade stalls, and a wax museum. The Palais Royal is also a good place to beg. The children hope that someone in the crowd will give them a couple of sous.

Pierrette likes the different characters in the puppet shows.

Moving lantern slide from a magic lantern (an early type of projector)

Lever for moving slide and making the boat roll

String puppets

Keeping a lookout
At the market, I look out for the watchman. He will chase us away if he sees us.

Playing
Our favorite game is called "follow-my-leader." We play by the Seine River.

Acrobatics
Joseph likes to copy the acrobats. He can even walk on his hands!

Palais Royal

Puppet theater

Acrobat

Juggler

At the Palais Royal, Pierrette and Joseph like to watch the entertainers.

Sunday school
I don't go to school, but on Sundays I go to Sunday School at Saint Mary's Church. My mother taught me to read, so I can enjoy the Bible stories.

Bath time
Once a week, I have to have a bath. My sister puts the metal bath in the kitchen and heats water in a pot on the stove.

Growing Up in Industrial Britain

It is 1840 and Anne and her older sister are living with their father in the new station house at Edge Hill, near Liverpool. The Liverpool to Manchester railroad is the first passenger railroad in the world, and Anne's father, George, is the station master.

A goods depot
Edge Hill is a goods depot. Cotton, flour, oatmeal, and even pigs are brought to the station for shipment to Manchester.

Anne
Anne wears a cotton dress with petticoats and long pantaloons underneath. When Anne's mother died, she left Anne her woolen shawl.

Pocket watch

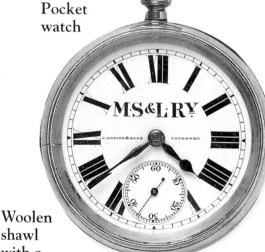

Woolen shawl with a Paisley pattern

The early train
Anne and her father get up at 6:00 a.m. At 7:05 a.m. exactly, the first train, The Lion, roars out of the tunnel. Steam hisses from the wheels and smoke belches from the funnel. Anne helps the first-class passengers onto the train.

Steam engine

On time
Anne's father must maintain the train timetable. He checks his pocket watch to make sure the trains do not run early or late.

Telling the time
Sometimes father lets me set his pocket watch. I have to set the time by the station clock.

Keeping the books
Father is teaching me to copy his accounts into ledgers, using a style of handwriting called copperplate. I must be careful not to spill the ink!

36

Darning
I help my sister mend our clothes. I darn my sister's stockings and my father's socks. New clothes are expensive.

Writing a letter
Every week, my father writes a letter to my aunt in Liverpool. He lets me stick the stamp on the envelope. Until recently, we didn't use stamps. The receiver had to pay for the letter.

At home
Anne helps her older sister with the housework. While her sister irons, Anne fills a pot with water to scrub the kitchen floor.

Iron

Hot coals are put inside the iron to heat it.

Penny black stamp

A penny black
Anne sticks a penny black stamp on her father's letter. This was the first postage stamp in the world. It shows Queen Victoria.

The fireman stokes the fire in the engine.

The guard sits on the front car. He blows a bugle when the train is about to go.

Luggage

Cars

Platform

Deliveries of flour and oatmeal wait to be loaded onto the train.

The signalman uses his hands to tell drivers to slow down or stop. At night he uses a lantern.

Coal is stored in a tender and used to fuel the train engines.

Talking to the train drivers
I tell the drivers that I want to drive a train one day, but father says women don't drive trains. He hopes I shall marry a railroad clerk or earn a living as a housemaid.

Playing games
In the evenings, I like to play dominoes or checkers with my father or sister.

Growing Up on the American Plains

It is 1850 on the banks of the Missouri River. Ohe-tika-wi, a girl of the Dakota people, and her family are following teeming herds of buffalo across the Great Plains. Ohe-tika-wi works with her mother and the other Dakota women in the camp.

Missouri River

The Great Plains

Ohe-tika-wi and her family cross the Great Plains on horseback. They have no permanent home, but set up camp with the rest of their tribe as they travel to hunt buffalo.

Ohe-tika-wi

Ohe-tika-wi wears a buffalo-skin dress decorated with paint, quills, and beads. Her favorite toy is her doll.

Saddlebag decorated with beadwork

Buffalo-skin bag

When hunting, Ohe-tika-wi's father carries food in a buffalo-skin saddlebag that Ohe-tika-wi helped make.

Painted decoration on tepee

Living in tepees

Buffalo hides are ideal for making tepees – cool in summer, but tough enough to keep out the rain and the wind in winter.

Buffalo-skin doll with beadwork dress

Preparing a hide

Ohe-tika-wi is busy working in the camp, preparing a hide to make clothes. She pegs the skin to the ground and scrapes off any fat and hair until the skin is smooth.

Fire for cooking and warmth

Buffalo hide

Buffalo dance
I watch my father and the other men of our tribe performing a dance to bring the buffalo to our hunt. They wear buffalo-skin masks.

Sewing skills
Ohe-tika-wi is learning how to decorate buffalo skins. Her mother shows her how to sew multicolored beads and porcupine quills onto the leather.

Baby's amulet
Ohe-tika-wi's baby brother has an amulet in the form of a turtle. It was made by his grandmother.

Amulet
My brother's amulet holds his umbilical cord and will ward off evil spirits.

Open flap to let smoke through

Cradleboard decorated with colorful quillwork

Buffalo meat
We skin and cut up buffalo carcasses. We will eat some of the meat now. The rest is dried in the sun on wooden racks and stored for winter.

Buffalo-skin amulet decorated with beadwork

Learning to weave
Ohe-tika-wi finds weaving porcupine quills difficult. Her mother tells her that in time, she will become skillful, and learn to decorate moccasins and other clothing.

Cooking
My favorite meal is buffalo meat stew. The cooking pot is made from — you guessed it — the stomach of a buffalo!

Baby's cradleboard
Ohe-tika-wi's mother carries her baby in a cradleboard made from soft buffalo skins.

Porcupine quillwork moccasins

Polishing shoes
On Sundays we go to church. I have to polish my shoes, comb my hair, and put on my best clothes.

A new car
My dad is saving up to buy a Model T Ford. We've never owned a car before.

Growing up in 1920s America

It is 1925 and Jack is living with his mother, father, and sisters in Brooklyn, New York City. Jack is in fourth grade at school. On weekends and in the evenings, when he doesn't have much homework, he helps out in his father's drugstore.

Jack's home
Jack lives with his family on the fifth floor of a brownstone building in Brooklyn. From his window, he can see the Brooklyn Bridge and the many tall buildings (called skyscrapers) on Manhattan Island.

Jack
Jack wears shorts, long socks, a shirt, sweater, and cap. He has to wear glasses because he is near-sighted.

Cookies and peanut butter are sold at the drugstore.

Cookies

Jack's motorcycle
Jack saved up his money to buy a toy motorcycle. He likes to race it across his bedroom floor.

Peanut butter

Toy motorcycle and rider

Some people come to the drugstore to use the telephone.

Jack helps the customers.

The drugstore
The family drugstore is on a busy street. It sells medicine, but also soft drinks, sweets, and groceries. Jack earns some money by keeping the shelves stocked. His father makes up the prescriptions and his mother serves snacks and drinks. Sometimes friends come in just to chat or to listen to the baseball game on the radio.

Music
I play the cornet in my school band. We are going to play in the Independence Day parade on the Fourth of July. I practice in my bedroom.

Steel nibs for pens

Jack's ink pen

At school, Jack writes with an ink pen. He has to dip the nib into the ink every few seconds.

Ink pen

Jack's school

Jack goes to school in Brooklyn. He is a class monitor and has to check that all the children have clean hands. Jack's favorite subject is science, especially nature study, when his teacher takes the class to the park.

Jack collects leaves to study back at school.

Dancing
My sisters, Mary and Beth, are learning a dance called the Charleston that is all the rage. They drive me mad by playing the record over and over on the phonograph.

Loudspeaker

The drugstore radio

Jack is a fan of the New York Yankees baseball team and listens to their games on the drugstore radio.

Radio receiver

An autographed photo

Jack's sisters have an autographed photo of their favorite movie star, Rudolph Valentino.

The movies
Mary and Beth have promised to take me to the Roxy theater to see a comedy film starring Charlie Chaplin.

41

Children From the Past

The children in this book are imaginary characters, but their stories are based on facts. How do we know about life in the past? We use clues that people leave behind in buildings, paintings, written documents, books, and all sorts of objects – from tools to toys. Here you can find out how objects from the past can survive to the present day.

Roman marbles

Objects from the past
People often lose objects, throw them away, or pass them on to others. Here, a Roman boy drops a marble.

Hundreds of years ago, a Roman boy plays marbles with his friends.

Buried treasure
As houses are built or destroyed, objects lost hundreds of years ago are buried deep underground. People called archaeologists dig for these objects. Above, archaeologists find the marble that was lost in Roman times.

The marble is cleaned and restored and displayed in a museum.

Children in history
The timeline below shows you how long ago each child in this book lived. Some lived before the birth of Christ (BC); some lived afterward (AD). Where do you live on the timeline?

Hori	Lysander	Miao	Vitalinus	Asa	Bilal	Sancho
1200	500	130 BC	AD 120	950	1400	1450

Discovering the past

Historians examine different clues that people leave behind and explain what the clues mean in books and museums. By reading books and visiting museums, we can build up a picture of how people used to live.

Exhibit in a museum

Clues for tomorrow

Imagine people living in the future, trying to find out how you live today. What clues will you leave behind for them to find? Below are some examples. What objects do you have that might survive for hundreds of years?

Calculator

Mechanical toy

Personal stereo

Giovanna	Xochitl	Kumar	Ichiro	Wiliyati	Pierrette	Anne	Ohe-tika-wi	Jack	
1490	1500	1600	1650	1700	1789	1840	1850	1925	2000

Glossary

Note: Words in **bold type** refer to other words in the glossary.

1920s America
The 1920s in the United States of America, remembered as happy times because of the hardships of the economic depression that followed.

Aboriginal
Aboriginals are inhabitants of Australia. They were the first people to settle in the country about 40,000 years ago.

Ancient China
In 221 BC the Qin dynasty (family) united China and gave the country its name. At the time described in this book, China was ruled by the Han dynasty, which lasted from 206 BC to AD 220.

Ancient Egypt
The time when Egypt was ruled by the pharaohs (kings of ancient Egypt), from 3000 BC until Roman times.

Ancient Greece
The time from the first great civilization in Greece, the Minoan, beginning in about 2000 BC, to 30 BC, when the Romans began to extend their power in the Mediterranean.

Aztec
There had been 1,500 years of civilization in what is now called Mexico before the Aztecs became one of the most powerful peoples in the country in 1428. By 1521, Spanish conquistadors (conquerors) had defeated the Aztecs, ending their rule.

BC and AD
In many countries, years are counted from the birth of Jesus. BC stands for "Before Christ." BC years are counted backward from Christ's birth. AD stands for the Latin words "Anno Domini," meaning "In the year of our Lord." AD years are counted forward from Christ's birth.

Castle
Castles were fortresses built by kings and noblemen to defend their lands. Most were built between the 1000s and 1500s, during the period known in Europe as the Middle Ages.

Copperplate
A neat, simple handwriting style, written with pen and ink in Victorian Britain.

Dakota people
A people who live in North America. They were among the first people living in the country, over 10,000 years ago, long before European settlers arrived in the 1500s. The Dakota people were one of many tribes called the Sioux by other Native Americans and then by European settlers.

Dreamtime
A time when **Aboriginals** believe that their animal, plant, and human ancestors created the world and everything in it.

Fjord
A long, narrow inlet of the sea.

Hinduism
A very ancient religion, which is followed by the majority of people living in India. Hindus worship many gods, including Brahma, Vishnu, and Shiva.

Homer
An ancient Greek poet who is said to have written *The Iliad* and *The Odyssey*, two famous story poems.

Industrial Britain
The time of the Industrial **Revolution** in Britain, beginning in about 1760, when machines changed the way people lived.

Knight
A well-armed and armored soldier, trained in the art of fighting on horseback.

Legionaries
Much of the Roman army was made up of legions, each of about 5,000 men. The soldiers were called legionaries.

Madrigals
A song for two or more voices, sung in parts and without instruments.

Mali Empire
The West African territories on the edge of the Sahara Desert that were ruled by the Mansa, or king of the Mali, between 1230 and 1500.

Moghul India
The time when parts of India were ruled by the Moghul dynasty (family), from 1526 to 1858.

Pitjantjatjara
A group of Australian **Aboriginals**.

Renaissance
A time in European history of new learning and rediscovery of the arts and ideas of the ancient Greeks and Romans. It began in Italy in about 1300 and lasted more than 200 years. Renaissance means rebirth.

Revolution
A revolution is a period of great upheaval and change. The French Revolution lasted from 1789 to 1794 and led to a new form of government.

Roman Empire
The parts of Europe, North Africa, and the Middle East that were ruled by the Romans. The first settlement was built in Rome in about 753 BC; the Empire reached its greatest extent in AD 117; and in 395 it was split into two halves: the Western Empire ended in 476 and the Eastern in 1453.

Samurai
Warriors who served the emperors and later the **shoguns** of Japan.

Shogun
Emperors ruled Japan from 1185 to 1868, but real power lay with shoguns, or military leaders. In 1868, power was restored to the emperor.

Tea ceremony
The Japanese tea drinking ritual, based on Zen Buddhist religious principles.

Tokugawa Japan
The time when Japan was ruled by the Tokugawa dynasty (family) of **shoguns**, from 1603 to 1868.

Vikings or Norsemen
Warriors from Norway, Sweden, and Denmark who raided and settled in northern Europe, Greenland, Iceland, and Russia, from the 700s to 1000s.

A Guide to Pronunciation

Note: Syllables in capital letters are the stressed syllables. Japanese has no stressed syllables.

Bilal: bi-LAL
Bjorn: BE-yawn
Cerberus: SIR-ber-US
Chiton: KI-ton
Demetrius: de-MEET-tree-US
Edo: eh-doe
Francesco: fran-CHES-co
Gajpati: GAJ-pa-TEE
Genialis: GEN-ee-AR-lis
Giovanna: jov-VARN-na
Hakama: hah-kah-mah
Hori: HOR-ee
Hneftafl: HE-nef-TA-fl
Ichiro: ee-chee-ro
Jag Sobha: JARG so-BHA
Kabuto: kah-boo-toh
Katana: kah-tah-nah
Kumar: KOO-mar
Liu bo: loo BO
Lysander: LIE-san-DER
Miao: MEE-ow
Naginata: nah-gee-nah-tah
Ohe-tika-wi: O-he-TEE-ka-WEE
Piraeus: PIE-ray-US
Pitjantjatjara: PIT-jant-JAT-jar-a
Ungka: UNG-ka
Vitalinus: VEE-ta-LEE-nus
Wakan Tanka: WA-kan TAN-ka
Wakizashi: wah-kee-zah-she
Wiliyati: WIL-ee-YAR-tee
Xochitl: SHO-chi-TL

Acknowledgments

Dorling Kindersley would like to thank the following for their help in producing this book: Sophia Tampakopoulos and Andrea Needham for jacket design, Hilary Bird for the index, and Monica Byles.

Photography: Peter Anderson, Andy Crawford, Geoff Dann, Mike Dunning, Steve Gorton, Christi Graham, Peter Hayman, Dave King, Liz McAulay, David Murray, Nick Nicholls, Martin Norris, Stephen Oliver, Roger Phillips, Tim Ridley, Kate Warren, Paul Williams, and Michel Zabé.

Dorling Kindersley would like to thank the following for their kind permission to reproduce photographs:

The British Film Institute, The British Library, The British Museum, Museo Nacional de Antropología, Mexico City, The Museum of Mankind, National Museum of Denmark, The Pitt Rivers Museum, The Royal Museum of Scotland, Statens Historika Museum, Stockholm, Sweden, Viking Ship Museum, Oslo, Norway, and The Wallace Collection.

Picture agency credits: (a=above, b=below, c=center, l=left, r=right, t=top)
Ancient Art and Architecture Collection/Ronald Sheridan 20c, 31cr. **Archiv fur Kunst und Geschichte** front cover cra, 35tr. **Bridgeman Art Library**/Oriental Bronzes Ltd. 15cra, London; Private Collection 25tr. **BFI Stills, Posters & Designs** 41br.

British Museum 14bl, 14-15bc, 15br. **Moira Broadbent** 28c, 28bl. **Mary Evans Picture Library** 37tr. **Rebecca Hossack Gallery** 33tc. ©**Japan Archive** 30bl. **National Museum of Ireland** 19br. **Robert Opie Collection** back cover cr, front cover br, 7br, 40cl, 40clb, 40bl. **Axel Poignant Archive** 33cb, 33bc. **Rijksmuseum voor Volkenkunde** 20bl, 21tl. **Scala**/Museo Horne, Firenze 25br; Palazzo Devanzati, Firenze 24bc. **The Science Museum**/Science and Society Picture Library 37tc. **Victoria and Albert Museum** 4, 29tr, 34bl, 34c. **Paul Straker Welds** 41bl. **Werner Forman Archive** 39bc/Plains Indian Museum, BBHC, Cody, Wyoming, USA: The Bradford Collection back cover cl, 38bl, R.L. Anderson Collection front cover tc, 6bl, 39tr; Museum fur Volkerkunde, Berlin 38c, 39c; Private Collection 31bl; Private Collection, New York 30c. **York Archaeological Trust** 6br, 19cr.

Every effort has been made to trace the copyright holders. Dorling Kindersley apologizes for any unintentional omissions and would be pleased, in such cases, to add an acknowledgment in future editions.